An Enchanted Land
The Shawangunk Mountains

An Enchanted Land
The Shawangunk Mountains

John E. Winkler

North Country Books
Utica, New York

An Enchanted Land
The Shawangunk Mountains

Copyright © 2003
John E. Winkler

ISBN 0-925168-91-2

Color Separations by
Rainbow Digicolor Inc. Toronto
Printed and bound in Hong Kong, China
by Book Art Inc., Toronto

Cover: *Looking north from Napanoch Point,
near the southwestern edge of Minnewaska State Park.*
Back Cover: *Blueberry Run trail at the Peters Kill crossing
after an early winter snow storm*

NORTH COUNTRY BOOKS
311 Turner Street
Utica, New York 13501
315-735-4877

Dedication

This book is dedicated to all persons
with a deep appreciation and respect for Nature.

To all who have helped in preserving this beautiful
and wondrous land for present and future generations
to enjoy through recreation and education.

Contents

Kayackers on the Wallkill River at New Paltz. The prominent white cliffs of the Shawangunks in the Mohonk Preserve are seen in the background.

Acknowledgements

Without help from others, this book would have been difficult to complete. First, I would like to thank the following hikers who accompanied me on the many treks to the Shawangunks to take photographs: Eugene Brousseau, Dan D'Amour, Kathleen Gill, Walt Hayes, Peter Watrous, and Mike Whelan.

The following individuals and organizations helped with historical and technical information pertaining to the Shawangunks: Roger Baker (hang gliding); Basha Kill Area Association; Olive Boylan (historian, Munnsville Museum); Debbie Clifford (Mohonk Preserve); Larry Braun (Chairman, West Hudson North Trails Committee); Clark Galloway; Hatti Langsford (Minnewaska Preserve); Susan Lavelle; Carleton Mabee (Gardiner historian/ author); Mike Medley and Heidi Wagner (Nature Conservancy at Sam's Point); Joseph Richards (skydivers); Randy Strechert; Ruth Schottman (naturalist/ author); Marty Podskoch (Forest Fire Lookout Assoc.); and the NY-NJ Trail Conference.

The pen and ink sketches were drawn by Mike Whelan. A recent graduate of Oneonta State University, he has a bachelors degree in mass communication. He also studied Spanish and television production in Quito, Ecuador. He has worked for local television stations and production companies in the Albany, New York area, as well as produced and shot videos in South America and India.

The two "Ramblings" which appear in this book were written by a friend and neighbor, the late Carl W. Uschman. He greatly enjoyed drives to the country, which inspired him to write. Mr. Uschman lived all of his life in Schenectady, New York. He worked for the General Electric Company and the former ALCO Products before retiring. He died in 1971.

Kathleen Gill wrote the story, "Great Uncle Billy's Watch Fob" and did a tremendous amount of research on the expansion culvert found in the Basha Kill area, as well as researching Shawangunk folklore. She is a certified teacher and social worker. Ms. Gill is a professional storyteller and operates a storytelling business—The Story Walker Limited, which provides storytelling residencies and programs offering adults and children the art of telling their own family stories.

She has hiked the Long Trail (Vermont); the Northville-Lake Placid Trail (NY); the Appalachian Trail (Maine to Georgia); the Catskill 35; the Northeast 111; the winter 48 in New Hampshire; and is an Adirondack 46er both in summer and winter.

She has also hiked in Ireland, Scotland, Wales, Denmark, Iceland, Germany, Norway, Austria, Bulgaria, and Canada.

Four-Mile Camp, 1938

Berry picker cabin – Sam's Point Preserve

Introduction

I joined the Adirondack Mountain Club (ADK) in 1970 and quickly became very active in hiking, mostly in the Adirondacks. In 1976, I became a 46er after climbing all the Adirondack peaks over 4,000 feet. A fellow by the name of Eugene Brousseau was an active member in the ADK at that time. He and I became very good friends and he got me interested in photography and bushwhacking. I then went on to do what no one else had done, in modern times anyway, bushwhack all the Adirondack 46 peaks without using a trail or herd path. This took about five years to do.

In 1983, Gene introduced me to the Shawangunks. I was very impressed with its unique and beautiful scenery. I found it was a great alternative to hiking the Adirondacks and as time went on I did more and more hiking and later on mountain biking as well in this area.

After having two books of photographs published on the Adirondacks, *A Bushwhacker's View of the Adirondacks*, 1995 and *A Cherished Wilderness*, 1998, both by North Country Books, I began to compile photographs of the Shawangunks and decided to put together a pictorial review of this unique area in New York State.

Bushwhacking opportunities are scarce in the Shawangunks, mainly because the area is well covered by trails and carriage roads, or the land is private and posted. Due to the sensitive environment, bushwhacking is also discouraged and in some areas prohibited.

Rock climbers testing their skills on the northern end of the cliffs at the Trapps in the Mohonk Preserve

About the Shawangunks

The Shawangunk Mountains, commonly known as the "Gunks," is a sixty-mile-long ridge extending northeast to southwest from Rosendale, New York on the northeastern end, to High Point State Park, New Jersey on the southwestern end. The Gunks are not connected to, or part of, the Catskill Mountains as some people believe.

The ridge is divided into two sections. Between Rosendale and Ellenville it is known as the Northern Shawangunks and lies entirely within Ulster County. This area includes the Mohonk Mountain House Resort, Mohonk Preserve, Minnewaska State Park Preserve, and Sam's Point Preserve, formerly known as Ice Caves Mountain. In addition, there are three small forest preserve areas.

Between Ellenville and the New Jersey State line, in Sullivan and Orange Counties, it is known as the Southern Shawangunks. Although much of this land is in private ownership, there are 3,400 acres of state forest lands and 3,000 acres of public lands in and around the Basha Kill wetland.

The Shawangunk Ridge Trail (SRT) offers the hiker access along the entire southern section. Parts of the trail are routed below the summit ridge and sometimes along roadways.

The geology of the Gunks is unique, with its quartz conglomerate rocks and cliffs, smoothed and polished in places from the glaciers. Its thin layer of soil retains little moisture, therefore most areas are very dry during the summer months. During draughts, some areas are closed to visitors. There are five "skytop" lakes, all within the northern section, which are naturally acidic and have no fish. The Northern Shawangunks are widely recognized as one of the most important sites for biodiversity conservation in the northeastern United States.

One of the unique features of the Northern Shawangunks is its many ice caves. The Greater Ice Caves at Sam's Point Preserve is the largest and most dramatic. The snow and ice, which remain most of the summer, create an environment that enables lichens and vegetation, normally found farther north, to grow. Persons exploring this area are advised not to disturb any vegetation in this sensitive environment.

The Shawangunks are rich in history. Native Americans inhabited the area as early as 4,000 BC. Picking and selling blueberries was a major industry on the mountain from the late 1800s to 1950. Many of the old cabins still remain in Sam's Point Preserve.

Located in the southeastern part of the state, the climate of the Shawangunks is generally warmer than upstate or western areas of New York State. The warmest temperature on record occurred on August 9, 2001, when the thermometer reached 101° F. The coldest day was a chilly 24° F recorded on December 30, 1917. Snowfall is also less than in most other areas of New York state. The greatest snowfall to date in a twenty-four hour period occurred on December 14, 1917, with twenty-four inches, according to the records at the Mohonk Cooperative Weather Station which was established on January 1, 1896.

The topographical maps that cover the Shawangunks are the 7.5 minute series of Mohonk Lake, Kerhonkson, Gardiner, and Napanoch Point, for the northern section. The Ellenville, Wurtsboro, and Yankee Lake 7.5 minute series, covers the southern Shawangunks.

When entering Mohonk or Minnewaska State Park, maps of the respective areas are given with your day pass. There is also a four-part waterproof map set published jointly by the Mohonk Preserve and the New York-New Jersey Trail Conference, which covers all of the Northern Shawangunks; Mohonk Resort, Mohonk Preserve, Minnewaska State Park, and Sam's Point Preserve. The Long Path Guide Book (a NY-NJ Trail Conference publication) covers and describes the Shawangunk Ridge Trail (SRT) in its entirety, in addition to the Long Path (LP). The SRT from Wurtsboro south, is also an alternative Long Path route through Orange County.

Bonticou Crag from the Wallkill Valley Rail Trail between Rosendale and New Paltz

Vegetation and Wildlife

The Shawangunks contain a wide variety of trees, wildflowers, and shrubs. Along the ridgetop the vegetation varies quite extensively, while along the base of the mountain it remains fairly uniform.

On the northern end (Mohonk Preserve) there are many groves of tall hemlock and white pine. Oak, maple, and pitch pine are also common, and a few stands of virgin hemlock remain.

Further south along the ridgetop in Minnewaska State Park, birch, sassafras, black gum (tupelo), maple, pitch pine, and a variety of oak are common.

At Sam's Point Preserve, at the southern end of the Northern Shawangunks, the dwarf pitch pine is the dominant tree, and there are some hardwoods as well.

Along the Southern Shawangunk ridgetop more oak and maple are found and only a few areas of pitch pine.

Chestnut trees were once common throughout the area, but a blight in the early part of the twentieth century decimated them. Young saplings still can be found, but they too succumb to the blight before reaching maturity.

Mountain Laurel is the most common shrub found along the entire ridgetop. Blueberries are also found everywhere, but Minnewaska and Sam's Point have the heaviest concentrations. Wild cranberries are plentiful in the small acidic bogs along the High Point Carriageway near High Point.

Many animals and birds make their homes in the Shawangunks. Deer, bobcat, beaver, otter, and occasionally a black bear will be seen. Blue herons, hawks, and even a bald eagle can be found. A good place to view a variety of wildlife is in the Basha Kill Wetland Area.

A variety of non-venomous snakes live in the Gunks, but the area is best known for its two varieties of venomous snakes—Copperheads, which are relatively common, and the Timber Rattlesnake. The Timber Rattler is listed in New York State as a threatened species. It is illegal to harm, capture or kill them. Due to increasing development and shrinking habitat, it is almost certain that in the future its status will be downgraded to endangered.

These impressive snakes are slow reproducers. Females have only two to four litters per reproductive lifetime and the survival rate is seventy percent. These snakes are very large—up to forty-eight inches in length and three inches in diameter—and have a lifespan of up to thirty years.

A tan phase Timber Rattler. Due to its threatened status, I was asked not to reveal the location where the snake was encountered.

The Wallkill Valley Rail Trail begins on the Rosendale trestle, built in 1871, which spans the Rondout Creek and the remains of the old D&H Canal.

Wallkill Valley Rail Trail

Between Rosendale and two miles south of Gardiner, is a fifteen-mile multi-use rail trail, developed and maintained by the Wallkill Valley Rail Trail Association (WVRTA). The Wallkill Valley Railroad operated its trains along this route between 1871 and 1977, and in later years it was operated by the Conrail System.

A nice attraction along the trail, at Hugenot Street in New Paltz, is an hour-and-a-half walking tour of the city's historic district – home to one of America's oldest streets with buildings dating back to the late 1600s.

Another attraction, a quarter mile from the trail, at the Gardiner airport, is the sky-divers. On a nice day, up to one thousand divers can be viewed. Those with experience, jump from 13,500 feet while novices begin around 8,000 feet. Although a year-round sport when weather is favorable, only the experienced take to the skies from November to April.

Skydivers prepare to land at Gardiner airport.

From an overpass on the Wallkill Valley Rail Trail near New Paltz is a nice view of the Smiley Tower and Shawangunk Ridge (Mohonk Preserve).

Midway between New Paltz and Gardiner, along the Wallkill Valley Rail Trail, is a great view of the entire Northern Shawangunks from Sam's Point to Mohonk.

Chapter One

Mohonk Preserve and Mountain House Resort

Summerhouse near Mohonk Mountain House

Mohonk Preserve

Located along the Northern Shawangunk ridge, the Mohonk Preserve maintains over 6,400 acres of semi-wilderness lands which are home to a variety of rare and endangered plants and wildlife. The Preserve carries on the legacy the Smiley family started in 1869, when they began acquiring land on the ridge buffering their growing resort. The Preserve's mission is to protect this sensitive ecological complex, while providing for public recreation and education. While the Mohonk Preserve evolved from the Mohonk Mountain House Resort, it is an entirely separate organization. Both organizations share in protecting this National Historic Landscape.

The Preserve was initially established in 1963 by the Smiley family as the Mohonk Trust. In 1970, the U.S. Secretary of the Interior designated the Mohonk Mountain House and the Preserve landscape as a National Historic Landmark. In 1978 the Trust was renamed the Mohonk Preserve.

The Preserve is the largest member and visitor supported nature sanctuary in New York State. Visitors with a day pass and members have access to the Preserve lands, sunrise to sunset, every day of the year and can hike or bike onto neighboring Mohonk Mountain House lands or Minnewaska State Park. Educational programs are provided for all visitors, and members can attend free of charge or at a reduced rate.

Over 65 miles of carriage roads and hiking trails are within the Preserve, which is a day use area only. Monies collected from day users and memberships are used to protect and maintain the Preserve, support education, for stewardship, and for research programs.

The Mohonk Mountain House Resort, which maintains 2,200 acres, is surrounded by Preserve lands. The Victorian-style house is seven stories high with 75 guest rooms and overlooks Mohonk Lake. This National Historic Landmark is still operated by the Smiley family today.

The grounds feature beautiful gardens with a variety of flowers, trees, and shrubs; a barn museum which contains an array of old tools, vintage autos, trucks, and interesting Mohonk memorabilia. There is also a golf course, tennis courts, and the prominent Smiley Sky Top Tower. The tower was constructed in the early 1920s as a memorial to Albert K. Smiley. Visitors can take the stairs to the top of the tower for an impressive view. On a clear day, the Catskills, Berkshires, Taconics, and the Hudson Highlands can be seen. Sky Top tower was also used as a fire observatory for fifty years.

The prominwent tower and the magnificant cliffs of the Northern Shawangunks are visable from the New York State Thruway between New Paltz and Poughkeepsie. The tower is also seen from Route 209 south of Stone Ridge, as well as from many vantage points throughout the Preserve and Minnewaska State Park.

The cliffs in the Mohonk area are well known as one of the most popular and extensive rock climbing areas in the eastern United States.

Visitors are welcome at the Preserve's Visitor Center, located in the town of Gardiner along Routes 44/55. More than 150,000 people visit the Preserve each year.

Opposite page:
From a vantage point near the
Humpty Dumpty Carriage Road,
is a view looking southwest
towards Minnewaska State Park.

Looking west from the cliffs near Smiley Tower

Chimney Rock beneath Smiley Tower

Late autumn woods near the northeast terminus of the High Peters Kill Trail, Coxing Kill area, Mohonk Preserve

Rock Climbing

Rock climbing is one of the most popular activities in the Northern Shawangunks. Fritz Weissner, an emigrant from Germany, made the first ascent on Millbrook Mountain in 1935. It was he who discovered that the durable, hard, quartzite conglomerate rock of the Shawangunks offered dependable holds and an excellent place to rock climb.

Most of the rock climbing cliffs are located on the Mohonk Preserve. Minnewaska State Park allows rock climbing in the Peters Kill area only. Sam's Point Preserve does not allow rock climbing.

On the Mohonk Preserve, climbers have access to 1,000 climbing routes and five linear miles of cliff face. The Preserve has one of the best trained vertical rescue teams in the northeastern United States.

More than 50,000 climbers visit this internationally renowned world-class climbing area each year.

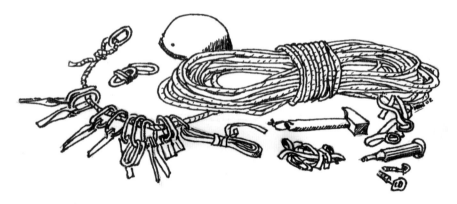

Rock climbing equipment 1960s

Rock climbers near Trapps Bridge

Experienced rock climbers on the cliffs of "Lost City," a popular climbing area near Coxing Kill, off the Clove Road

"Lost City," photographed from the High Peters Kill Trail in the Ronde Barre region of Mohonk Preserve

14

WILD BLEEDING HEARTS. This native perennial belongs to the poppy family and likes rocky woodlands like that of the Shawangunks. Blooming in summer, these were photographed in the Mohonk Preserve.

Mohonk Lake and the Resort Hotel from Eagle Cliff. One of the many gazebos around the lake can be seen at the left.

Clove Valley from the Undivided Lot Trail

Mohonk Mountain House Resort and its magnificent gardens

A beautiful clematis vine in the Mohonk Gardens

The spiderflower is a popular annual at Mohonk Gardens.

Below Smiley Tower, on The Crevice Trail, is an impressive view of the Hudson Valley.

A young man jumps a crevice on the rocks at "Lost City."

The Sky Top Tower at an elevation of 1,542 feet as seen from the Eagle Cliff Carriage Road

The Hudson Valley from Sky Top Tower

On a high point, just off the Old Minnewaska Trail near the junction of Laurel Ledge Carriage Road,
is still another view of the prominent Smiley Tower.

22

Moss covered wall on a tributary of the Coxing Kill between
Clove Road and the Old Minnewaska Trail

COMMON MILKWEED seeds, photographed in a field
near the Spring Farm Carriage Road

23

Looking north from 1,194-foot Bonticou Crag in winter

Looking northwest from Bonticou Crag, the Northeast Trail and Bonticou Carriage Road can be seen.

Picturesque Duck Pond is a popular destination for hikers and bikers.
Sky Top Tower can be seen atop the cliffs in the background.

View from Table Rocks looking north...

...and looking southwest

27

Looking northeast from Smiley Tower, towards Guyot Hill, old Sky Top Reservoir
is seen in the foreground; the Berkshire Mountains in the background.

Chapter Two

Minnewaska State Park Preserve

Lake Minnewaska and Resort Hotel—Early 1900s

Minnewaska State Park Preserve

Minnewaska State Park Preserve was created in 1970 when 6,725 acres were purchased from the Lake Minnewaska Resort, which included Lake Awosting, the largest of the "sky" lakes and Mud Pond. The remaining property was aquired in two separate purchases, one in 1977 and the other in 1986, which included Lake Minnewaska. The current size of the Preserve is now about 12,000 acres.

The stone house overlooking Lake Minnewaska was owned by the Phillips family, which operated the two resort hotels that were once popular with tourists. After the resort industry dropped off, the hotels were burned and torn down and the land was sold to the state. The Phillips retained lifetime rights to their private home on the property, but could not pass the home onto their children. The park's master plan calls for eventually turning the home into an educational and research facility. Built around 1980, the home contains a lot of the old lumber and lighting fixtures that were once part of the resort hotels.

Four prominent waterfalls are within the park. Stony Kill—the highest with a sheer drop of ninety feet, Rainbow Falls, Awosting Falls, and Peters Kill Falls.

Activities including bicycling, swimming, scuba diving, hiking, horseback riding, cross-country skiing, snowshoeing, picnicking, bird watching, and hunting. Rock climbing is permitted, with permit, only on the Lower Peters Kill Escarpment.

The park receives about 250,000 to 500,000 visitors each season, and the numbers have been increasing each year.

Opposite page:
The 300-foot cliffs of Millbrook Mountain,
as seen from the massive tallus fields below

Blueberry Run Trail at the Peters Kill crossing after an early winter snow storm

Lake Awosting from the east shore

Ice covered trees near Lake Minnewaska

The pink-flowered azalea, or PINXTER FLOWER, blooms in late May
and early June, before the leaves are fully expanded.

This large wetland area along Fly Brook between the Peters Kill and
Smiley Carriage Roads, north of Lake Awosting is trailless.

Huntington Ravine near Rainbow Falls

The Hudson Valley from atop Millbrook Mountain

Mud Pond in early winter

Mud Pond, formerly known as Haseco Lake, is the smallest of the five "sky" lakes.
It is three-quarters of a mile west of Lake Awosting.

A view looking east from Beacon Hill. The Peters Kill area is in the foreground;
the Trapps and the Smiley Tower are in the background.

40

Tree branches, heavy with frozen mist and snow, at the base of Awosting Falls

The Peters Kill below Awosting Falls

A short distance from Minnewaska's main entrance is Awosting Falls.
The 60-foot falls was photographed in January.

With a sheer drop of 90 feet, Stony Brook Falls
is the highest in Minnewaska State Park.

Ice on Litchfield Ledge. The Awosting Carriage Road along the ledge's base
is often impassable during winter due to icy conditions.

The carriage road beneath Castle Point in January

44

A view of Gertrude's Nose looking towards Kempton Ledge

Hidden Pond near the north corner of Minnewaska State Park is difficult to find because of old and faintly marked trails.

Beautiful ice formations at the base of Rainbow Falls

Viewed from Millbrook Mountain, early morning fog rises from the valley

View from a rock outcropping near the carriage road between Awosting Falls
and Lyon Road looking east towards Mohonk Preserve

48

Fly Brook, near the Stony Kill Carriage Road crossing

A view of the Hudson Valley from Gertrude's Nose

Lake Minnewaska after a winter ice storm

Lake Awosting, 1.2 miles long and up to ninety feet deep, is the largest of the five sky lakes.
Sam's Point Preserve is the long ridge seen in the background.

Gertrude's Nose as seen from the Castle Point Carriage Road

A view looking north from one of many open areas in the region south of Hidden Pond.
Rondout Valley and the Catskill Mountains are in the background.

From the top of Millbrook Mountain, looking northeast, the Bayards,
Near Trapps, Trapps, and the Smiley Tower are seen.

The northeast end of Millbrook Mountain as seen from the tallus fields

54

Mountain bikers rest at Lake Awostina

From Margaret Cliff, Castle Point (top) and Hamilton Point (at bottom) are viewed in the distance.

Looking north toward the Catskills, between Battlement Terrace and Castle Point, is this striking view of the unique Shawangunk landscape.

Gertrude's Nose and the Hudson Valley as seen from Castle Point. In the distance
are the southern Berkshires and the mountains of western Connecticut.

MOUNTAIN LAUREL, an evergreen shrub, is abundant throughout the Shawangunks. Flowering in June and having a height of between three and eight feet, the showy flowers were photographed along the Gertrude's Nose Trail.

Lake Minnewaska in June, with the mountain laurel in bloom

This Old Road

It was Great Grandfather,
Who laboriously hacked this old carriage road out of the forest,
With the help of Old Nell and Big Tom,
The two sturdy equines borrowed from their plowing chores.

No one could have known,
That long after the utilitarian mission of those pioneering days ceased,
The pleasures this ancient lane would afford
To latter-day wanderers,
In search of something which only open spaces could provide.

Now rocky and partly obscured by the growth of young saplings,
Beside the steady splash of water,
O'er the diminutive rock escarpments;

As to call out through the sylvan silence,
To all who travel this way,
In the secluded woodlands,
To the accompaniment of feathered songsters;

That another day has ended,
And all should return home to rest,
In the quiet evening hour.

In meditation we realize,
It was our elders,
Who created this passage through the wilderness,
And brought to fruition,
A vision for all to behold,
And cherish forever.

—C. W. Uschman

Old Smiley Carriage Road near the Stony Kill

A view looking north from Napanoch Point, near the southwestern edge of Minnewaska State Park.
Since this area is more remote, it sees less visitors than other areas of the park.

The SASSAFRAS TREE, with its distinctive mitten-shaped leaves, is quite common throughout the Shawangunks.

An autumn reflection on a trailless section of the Peters Kill at the eastern
boundary of Minnewaska Park, a half-mile south of Hidden Pond

Chapter Three

Sam's Point Preserve

A fifty-foot steel fire tower at High Point was constructed in 1919. Closed in 1972, the tower was removed in 1988.

Sam's Point Preserve

In 1997, the Open Space Institute, a non-profit organization dedicated to preserving natural landscapes, acquired 4,600 acres now known as Sam's Point Dwarf Pine Ridge Preserve—previously known as Ice Caves Mountain which was a commercial tourist attraction. The caves were closed for several years, while the Nature Conservancy, which manages Sam's Point Preserve, renovated the walkways and stairs. The caves were re-opened to hikers in the summer of 2004. The Conservancy has given it the Last Great Place designation for National Conservation priorities.

On the Ellenville side of the mountain are more ice caves, known as the Greater Ice Caves. The deep cool rocky crevices of the ice caves create moist micro-climates that are home to several rare plant species, mosses, and lichens. The cliffs contain many raven nesting sites. Along the High Point Road are many undrained acidic and nutrient poor bogs, an ideal environment for the many wild cranberries found here.

A significant feature within the preserve is the Dwarf Pitch Pine Barrens. While other pitch pine barrens exist in the state and elsewhere, no where else do these globally rare dwarfted and stunted pitch pine exist on a ridgetop bedrock like those of Sam's Point Preserve.

Activities include hiking, bird watching, snowshoeing and cross-country skiing, and biking.

Lake Maratanza, at an elevation of 2,250 feet, is the highest and second largest of the sky lakes. In the 1960s it was dredged to make it deeper and it is a back-up water supply for Ellenville. Swimming and boating are prohibited.

The Long Path (LP), which starts at the western end of the George Washington Bridge and continues north to Altamont, extends through Sam's Point. A loss of land easement between Verkeerder Kill Falls and Mud Pond created a gap in the path here. Late in 2002, a major relocation has been proposed for the Long Path in this area, according to the Long Path Committee.

The Nature Conservancy coordinated hundreds of volunteer hours working on the trails in this area. The shallow soils are highly susceptible to erosion and are easily impacted by off-trail use.

The Old Stone Church at Cragsmoor, Chapel of the Holy Name, is a beautiful old landmark worth visiting. The church, constructed in 1895 with stone from the mountain, has been restored and holds services and weddings.

Opposite Page:
Lake Maratanza

The Verkeerder Kill upstream from the falls

The ridge from Sam's Point to the radio towers near Lake Maratanza offers
continuous views looking south to Sam's Point and Walker Valley.

RHODODENDRON bloom in mid-July. This shrub, with a height of up to 25 feet, is found along moist stream banks throughout the Gunks. Photographed in South Gulley

The 72-foot high Verkeerder Kill Falls as seen from the gorge below

70

The Badlands – A Mystical Forest

The Badlands is an area of 1,600 acres east of High Point at an elevation of 2,100 to 2,200 feet. It is one of the largest trailless sections in the Northern Shawangunks. Vast stretches of this land are dominated by dwarf pitch pines, growing to a maximum height of only five feet. The rest of the area is home to twisted scrub oak, birch, black gum or tupelo, maple, and sassafras trees. Between the rocky areas, low blueberry bushes cover much of the ground. Due to the elevation and exposure, it is almost always quite windy here.

The Badlands is like a Mystical Forest where one can imagine seeing an elf, leprechaun, or even a fairy princess! The stunted trees in countless wierd shapes and the unique rock formations all make this a fascinating place to explore.

The Mystical Badlands

One of the many artistic-looking tree skeletons found in the Badlands

The blueberry bushes turn a brilliant crimson in autumn in the Badlands.

Hudson Valley and the Berkshires as seen from Sam's Point in mid-winter

Lake Maratanza in winter

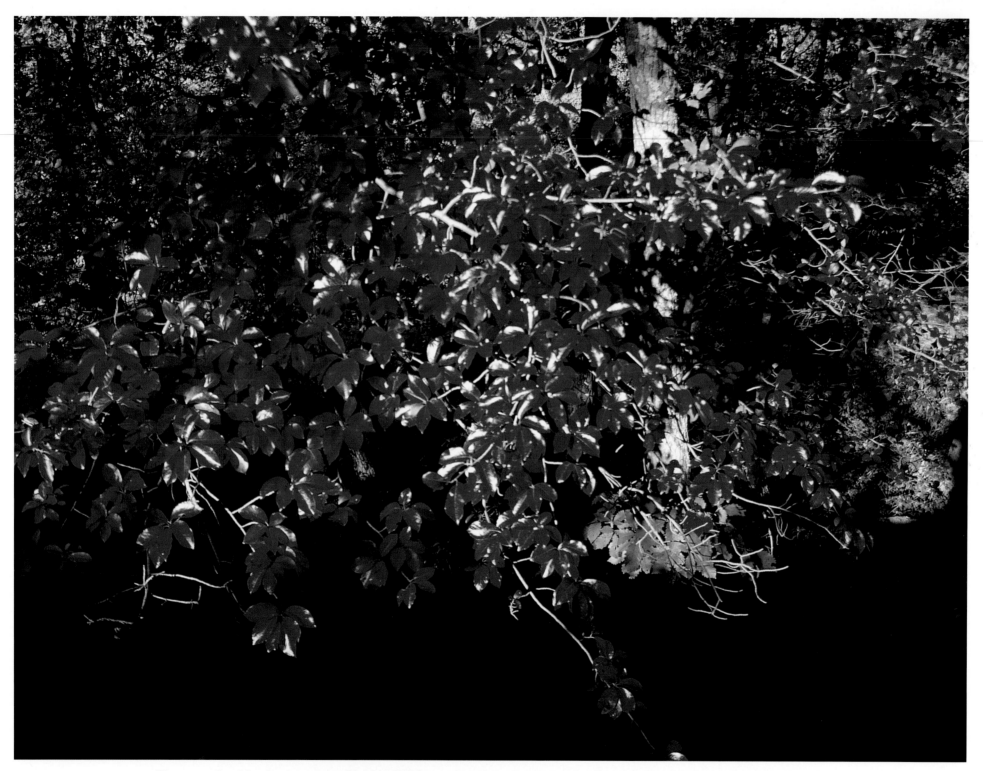

The smooth, shiny leaves of the BLACK GUM tree, found in abundance in Minnewaska and Sam's Point Preserves, turn a brilliant crimson in autumn. Birds enjoy its dark blue-black fruit.

From High Point, looking northward towards the Catskill Mountains.
The foreground is made up entirely of dwarf pitch pine.

The Nature Conservancy improved and cleared the half-mile trail down to Indian Rock.

A nice view of Mount Meenahga from the trail to Indian Rock, a mile north of Lake Maratanza off the High Point Carriage Road. The Pocono Mountains of Pennsylvania, can be seen in the background.

Mud Pond as seen from the Crags

SHEEP LAUREL, a low evergreen shrub with
pink flowers, blooms in June and July.

Trail to Verkeerder Kill Falls in the fall

A striking view of the Hudson Valley from Sam's Point

A view from the Pine Barrens, near the Verkeerder Kill Trail, Lake Awosting is visible in the background, as well as Castle Point and Gertrude's Nose. Mid-picture is the Verkeerder Kill Valley and the Crags.

Rock escarpment along the trail from Verkeerder Kill Falls to High Point, adjacent to the Badlands

Hikers carefully choose their footing in a bushwhack down the Louis Ravine.

A view looking south by the Ice Caves at Sam's Point

The Greater Ice Caves on the Ellenville side of Sam's Point Preserve

This snow pit on the south end of the Greater
Ice Caves was photographed in mid-July.

Mid-section of the Greater Ice Caves

87

The cool air at the bottom and the moist air above the caves often creates a fog line and a unique ecological environment. The Southern end of the caves is pictured above.

Northern end of the caves near Shingle Gulley

88

Bear Hill Nature Preserve

The Bear Hill Nature Preserve at Cragsmoor, off of Dellenbaugh Road, is owned by the Cragsmoor Free Library and maintained by the Cragsmoor Association. Opened in 1978, the half-mile trail to the viewing point is through private land with public access. At an elevation of 1,950 feet it is the last point southward on the Northern Shawangunk Ridge.

Looking west from Bear Hill, Spring Glen and the Sandburg Creek Valley can be seen in the distance.

Hang Gliding

Cragsmoor, the southwestern terminus of the Northern Shawangunks, is where hang gliders take to the skies in their colorful gliders. Using this site since the mid-1970s, they cruise the air currents year round, ideally when there is a northwest wind of ten to fifteen miles per hour.

Taking off from the launch site at 1,100 feet above the valley, near Route 52, the average cruise is between 2,500 to 8,000 feet. The highest known was at 10,500 feet. Most land in the valley below, near Ellenville, but some have travelled more than 100 miles into Connecticut. The average stay aloft is one-and-a-half to two hours, with some gliders staying up for as long as seven hours.

An excellent place to view the hang gliders is along Route 52, just below the launch site.

Chapter Four

Southern Shawangunks

Bald Eagle in the Basha Kill wetland

The Southern Shawangunks

The Shawangunk Ridge between Ellenville and the New Jersey state line is known as the Southern Shawangunks. This area is often overlooked since most people are more familiar with the popular Mohonk, Minnewaska, and Sam's Point Preserves in the Northern Shawangunks.

This thirty-five mile stretch has a trail the entire length called the Shawangunk Ridge Trail (SRT). It is also the route of the popular Long Path (LP). Completed in 1996, it has many access points and offers many fine views.

To protect the land from overdevelopment, several important tracts of land including the 1,400-acre Shawangunk State Forest, the 2,000-acre Wurtsboro State Forest, and 3,000 acres of wetlands an uplands known as the Basha Kill Wildlife Management Area have been acquired by the State of New York, using monies from the Environmental Bond Act.

Near Wurtsboro you can see the red and white Roosa Gap Fire Tower atop the 1,500-foot ridge. No longer in use, it was one of three such towers protecting the Shawangunks from fires. Established in 1948, the forty-seven-foot structure provided a view of the forests below the High Point and Mohonk Towers. During the 1940s and 50s, many fires in the area were caused from hot cinders that came from the steam engines on the Ontario and Western (O&W) railroad. Today, the tower is fenced off and is rented by the Sullivan County DPW.

From the Wurtsboro Ridge, one can watch glider planes cruising the airways. Wurtsboro Airport, which opened in 1927 was the first airport in the U.S. to introduce this popular sport.

At the base of the ridge, between Wurtsboro and Westbrookville is the Basha Kill wetland. Four and a half miles long and a half mile wide, these 3,000 acres provide for hiking, biking, bird watching, fishing, canoeing, and hunting. Picnicing areas are also available. It is the largest fresh water wetland in southeastern New York State. The SRT/LP traverses the entire length of the east shore of the wetland using the old NY O&W railbed. There are several stands for bird watching along the shoreline.

Located in the valley adjacent to the Shawangunk Ridge at Mamakating, is a hike and bike path in the D&H Linear Park. Using the old tow path that was once used by mules to pull the canal boats during the 1800s, this four and a half mile trail not only offers nice views of the ridge, but there are many wildflowers and birds to view along the way.

Opposite Page:
The Basha Kill wetland

Looking west across Shin Hollow from the Shawangunk Ridge two and a half miles north at Hathorn Lake

Looking east, an unusual rock formation near the
northern end of the Southern Shawangunks

The Shawangunk Ridge Trail passes many streams,
such as this one south of Otisville.

The Basha Kill

One of the most interesting and important areas in the Southern Shawangunks is the Basha Kill Wildlife Management Area, near Westbrookville. In the early 1970s the State of New York purchased the land and the Department of Environmental Conservation built a permanent dam on the Basha Kill above the Pine Kill, creating the wetland and stable water levels.

Muskrat, beaver, and otter are frequently seen mammals in the marsh. Ducks, osprey, bald eagles, and two-hundred-twenty species of birds, thirty species of fish, as well as forty species of amphibians and reptiles inhabit the area. About two hundred species of wildflowers can be found in the Kill and the surrounding woodlands.

The Basha Kill Area Association founded in 1972, is dedicated to preserving this beautiful area and protecting it from ecological degradation and promoting educational programs on the environment.

The wetland area, besides offering beautiful scenery, is a great place to watch sunrises, sunsets, stargaze, and to explore the night sky.

Otter

Mallard ducks in the Basha Kill wetland

The Basha Kill wetland in early spring

Autumn reflection seen from lookout stand #9 in the Basha Kill

In early summer, ducks can be seen with their young. The Shawangunk Ridge is in the background.
The arrowhead and pickerelweed will fill in most of the waterway by mid-summer.

Sunset over the Basha Kill

From the Wurtsboro Ridge, near Roosa Gap, scrub oak have replaced
the pitch pine. The Basha Kill wetland can be seen at back left.

Here at Hathorn Lake, the Shawangunk Ridge Trail traverses U.S. Route 6 for a short distance before going under I-84, then heads south to High Point, New Jersey, the southern terminus.

The Hudson Valley and I-84 from the ridge top one mile north of Hathorn Lake

Another mountaintop bog, Mud Pond, is seen along the Shawangunk Ridge Trail, five-and-a-half miles north of High Point, New Jersey and three miles south of I-84.

Port Jervis, the Delaware River, and the Poconos of Pennsylvania are seen here just before
the Shawangunk Ridge Trail enters New York State from High Point, New Jersey.

The CARDINAL FLOWER can be found in wet areas near streams and bogs like the Basha Kill. Blooming in August, it has brilliant scarlet-red flowers.

Legends and Mysteries

With human beings inhabiting the Shawangunks for the last 6,000 years, it's no wonder that the area holds much history, folklore, and legend.

One popular legend is how Sam's Point got its name. A 1700s frontiersman named Samuel Gonsalus is said to have jumped off the precipice to elude a party of Indians who were in pursuit. His fall was supposedly cushioned by the thick vegetation below.

One of the most notorious mysteries is an inscription which appears on a rock near the junction of the Verkeerder Kill Falls and High Point Trail, near the Crags. It reads: WHO AMONG US SHALL DWELL WITH EVERLASTING BURNINGS. Etched in professional lettering, weathered but still readable, it has been there since the early part of the twentieth century. No one knows who or why it was inscribed.

While doing a bushwhack of the upper Verkeerder Kill Basin, a vast trailless region that separates Sam's Point from the Badlands, several companions and myself discovered our own mystery.

A short distance above the Verkeerder Kill Falls, where we started the bushwhack, we found a nice swimming hole obviously known to others because of a well-worn path leading up to it. But from there on, we were on our own. The stream was pretty and the off-and-on open areas gave us views of the cliffs which line the southwestern edge of the Badlands.

After the stream ended we were fortunate enough to stumble unto an old tote road. It was there we discovered, sitting in the middle of nowhere, the mysterious piece of machinery pictured at right. Having a large basket on the front end, it somewhat resembled a supermarket shopping cart. At the rear were two handles and a place for a motor to drive it. The motor had been removed long ago. The rest of the cart was intact but rusty.

It was obviously abandoned many decades ago, since the vegetation had grown up around it. Appearing to be used as a plow of some kind, the heavy duty basket may have been used to haul rocks. It looks to be homemade, probably from the berry pickers who inhabited the area at that time. The 14-inch auto or truck tires were still fully inflated after all this time... top of the line white walls no less! We dubbed it "The motorized shopping cart."

From here the overgrown, but walkable, tote road gave us a way out of the basin to the High Point Carriage Road. It would have been impossible to continue without it as the pitch pine thickets were nearly impenerable.

I'm sure there are many more mysteries tucked away in this Enchanted Land. For the Shawangunks hold a charm and fascination unmatched anywhere else.

The expansion culvert along the eastern shore of the Basha Kill, looks about the same now as it did nearly one hundred years ago. The trains are long gone, and the railbed is now part of the Shawangunk Ridge Trail/Long Path.

A Mystery in History Solved

Railroads are an important part of Shawangunk history. So discovering yet another link in this historic chain was not unusual.

While taking photographs along the Basha Kill, I spotted a fascinating culvert underneath the east shore trail. Now, you might ask, why is an old rusty culvert of any interest when there is so much wildlife, flowers, and scenery to study?

This culvert was so unusual and well preserved that it prompted some research. The inscription on the iron plate surrounding it reads: NY O&W RR—SPERRY PERFECTION—Munnsville Plow Co.,—Munnsville, NY—pat. 05. The trail uses the former railbed of the old New York Ontario and Western Railroad which operated here from around 1880 to 1957.

These culverts, called expansion culverts, were invented by Mr. S. E. Sperry and manufactured at the foundry he incorporated in 1893—The Munnsville Plow Company of Munnsville, New York in Madison County. These distinctive culverts were used under roadways and on the O&W Railroad, a spur of which ran through Munnsville. The company manufactured many types of agricultural implements. Fire destroyed the original building in 1920, and in 1927 the company filed for bankruptcy.

The Fryer Memorial Museum in Munnsville has many of the foundry's items on display, including one of the expansion culverts. The museum's historian didn't think any of these culverts still existed in the ground.

A little diversion here, but an interesting one to say the least. For who knows, it might be on your travels and explorations of this Enchanted Land—The Shawangunk Mountains—who will uncover another piece of overlooked history or even solve one of its mysteries.

Sam's Point Preserve in winter, photographed from the shore of Lake Maratanza

110

Great Uncle Billy's Watch Fob

A Shawangunk Folklore Story

Great Uncle Billy was ten years old the first time he saw the white man and the Indian come across their fields from the wood-lot. The white man stopped and talked with his father. Billy was very surprised when his father left the field and took both men down to the barn.

He noticed the white man carried a coarse cloth sack across his shoulder, while the Indian carried a bundle of tanned hides. His father returned to the field alone.

Billy had a lot of questions, but held his tongue. He had asked before about the mountains, and his father had told him that they were called the Shawangunk Mountains. He said, "Those Shawangunks are full of gypsies and outlaws. None of the land up there is any good for farming." Billy just knew his father wouldn't tell him a thing about the strangers who came down from the mountain.

After his barn chores were finished, he asked his mother about the strangers. She said the white man was a hermit, the Indian was his friend and they lived up on the mountain. He started to ask more, but mother rebuked. After dinner that night, his mother packed food in a basket and brought it to the barn.

Great Uncle Billy said when he came down to the kitchen the next morning, he found his father eating breakfast. Father never ate until the morning milking was done. He told him, "Today, the morning chores are all yours. I will be back at noon."

He helped his father harness up the horses and hitch them to the wagon. His father and the hermit loaded the wagon with the hermit's bag and the bundle of deer hides and drove off.

The Indian went back into the barn, climbed to the loft and watched Billy do his chores. Billy remembered that it took him a long time, working alone, to care for all the animals. He had just finished when his mother called him to dinner. As he left the barn, his father and the hermit came back from town. Billy could see there were two large cloth bags in the wagon.

The Indian then came out of the barn and took one of the large bags from the wagon and the hermit took the other. His mother ran from the house and handed each of them a small sack of food. Both nodded to her. Each man shouldered his bag and walked across the fields, back towards the mountains.

Great Uncle Billy said his parents' silence about these guests just about drove him crazy. He wondered if they were the gypsies or outlaws that lived up on the mountain. He lay awake that night in bed and tried to imagine what it would be like to live in the mountains, when suddenly he heard some horses clatter up the lane and turn into the barnyard.

Some men called to his father. They were asking all kinds of questions about the hermit. Great Uncle Billy was shocked to hear his father lie to these men who were their neighbors. His father said, "That man came by right after breakfast, he must be a trapper or hunter. He asked for a ride to town. I could see he had a large pile of hides, so I gave him a ride. I don't know anything about what his business was. Maybe he traded the hides at the store for supplies. I attended to my own business, but did give him a ride back from town. He asked me to stop along the road, and he got out and went back into the woods. I don't know where he is now."

When the men rode off, his father shut the door. He heard him say to his mother, "It's no ones business what that old man does."

His mother replied, "That's true."

For the next four years toward the end of each September, when the Shawangunks were starting to don their calico garb, the white man and the Indian would come to the farm. Each time the same thing happened, including the men riding out to question Father.

The fourth visit was the last time he would ever see the white man

It was during that visit, that Great Uncle Billy saw a small, shinny odded-shaped pebble next to the feedbox. He thought the white man must have snagged his bag on a nailhead which had popped up on the edge of the feedbox. Having never seen a pebble like that before, he put it into his pocket.

Suddenly, the Indian climbed down from the loft and left the barn. He watched the Indian stay close to the stonewall fence until he reached the gate, crossed the road and went into the woods. Shortly, their neighbors rode into the barnyard and called out for his father. Billy said from the way his mother acted, she believed they knew father was in town with the hermit. He overheard his mother say, "We needed some supplies, so he went to town."

They said they would wait. His mother did not offer them coffee or ask them inside. Instead she said, "I have chores," and went back into the kitchen.

Just before noon, his father drove into the yard alone. He had some boxes in the wagon. The men wanted to know about the white man.

Father replied, "I've told you before, once in awhile I see him by the road. I give him a ride into town and if he is ready to leave when I am, I give him a ride back. He tells me where to stop along the road. I do, and he goes back into the woods."

The men seemed dissatisfied. Father unloaded the boxes and brought them to the porch. The men could see that there was nothing in those boxes except food stuff. Looking angry, the men left.

That fall, his father took sick with a high fever. His father had become so weak that he couldn't work the farm. Great Uncle Billy was only fourteen and couldn't keep up with all the farm work. His younger brother, who was shorter than the tools, was really too young to be of much help. He pitched in, but the work was just too much. They couldn't get all the crops harvested or enough wood cut before the first killing frost.

Billy said he could hear his parents talk, as he lay in bed, about these troubled times. His father was concerned that they might lose the farm if they didn't sell the cows or the second team of horses.

Billy was also worried about the farm and was still awake that November night, when he heard a tapping on his window. He looked out and saw the Indian, so he opened the window. The Indian motioned for him to come. Billy dressed warmly, climbed out and followed him.

At the edge of their fields, the Indian took Billy's scarf off of his neck and blindfolded him. He said it seemed like only a short time before the Indian took the blindfold off. He had led him to the base of the Shawangunks. The Indian started to climb up a faint path and Billy followed. The path ended just below the crown of trees at a cave. The Indian lit a lantern and they went inside.

The Indian pointed to a wall, which had a yellow streak in it and handed Billy a pickaxe. He swung the pickaxe at the yellow streak. Soon he had a tiny pile of yellow pebbles and dust. Billy watched as the Indian took a red leather pouch from a beam and filled it with the pebbles and dust. Pulling the strings of the pouch tightly, he hung the bag around Great Uncle Billy's neck. Then they left the cave.

Billy followed the Indian along a different ledge back down to the base of the mountain. Once again he was blindfolded. This time when his blindfold was removed he was under his window. He climbed inside and as he shut the window, he saw the Indian melt back into the shadows.

He fingered the bag and knew it was full of gold. He lay down on his bed and fell asleep. The next morning at breakfast, he told his mother and father about his adventure, and handed them the red pouch. His father told him to say nothing about this, ever. (And he didn't until his father and mother had been dead for many years).

The gold in that red pouch saved the farm.

Every November Billy would stand in the western fields, staring at the Shawangunks. Sometimes he thought he could see a dim bobbing light shinning from the cave, but could never place its location.

Great Uncle Billy told me he never looked too hard for that mine, but that some people in town did. He thought one or two of them might have found it because they never came back from their treasure hunt. His father had told him that the Shawangunk Mountains guard their lost mines. Billy would add that, even today, people don't often come back from treasure hunting in those mountains.

All the gold he ever found was that nugget next to the feedbox. He kept it hidden until he was an adult. Only after his father died, and his mother gave him his father's watch, did he take the nugget out of the house. He took it to a jeweler in Kingston who made him a watch fob. He hung the watch from it and was delighted to show it off.

Maybe he didn't leave us a lot of gold, but he left us one treasure— the story of his watch fob.

—Kathleen Gill